ORCH

Claire Masset

SHIRE PUBLICATIONS

Published in Great Britain in 2012 by Shire Publications
Ltd, Midland House, West Way, Botley, Oxford OX2 0PH,
United Kingdom.

44-02 23rd Street, Suite 219, Long Island City, NY 11101,
USA.

E-mail: shire@shirebooks.co.uk   www.shirebooks.co.uk

© 2012 Claire Masset.

Every attempt has been made by the Publishers to secure
the appropriate permissions for materials reproduced in
this book. If there has been any oversight we will be happy
to rectify the situation and a written submission should be
made to the Publishers.

A CIP catalogue record for this book is available from the
British Library.

Shire Library no. 632.   ISBN-13: 978 0 74780 838 1

Claire Masset has asserted her right under the Copyright,
Designs and Patents Act, 1988, to be identified as the
author of this book.

Designed by Tony Truscott Designs, Sussex, UK
and typeset in Perpetua and Gill Sans.

Printed in China through Worldprint Ltd.

12 13 14 15 16   10 9 8 7 6 5 4 3 2 1

COVER IMAGE
An apple orchard in Kent displays its bounty on a sunny
autumn morning.

TITLE PAGE IMAGE
This Art Deco print is delightfully captioned: 'The boys were
in the orchard as busy as three bees.'

CONTENTS PAGE IMAGE
An apple orchard in the village of Putley in Herefordshire,
which since Roman times has been a prime site for fruit
growing.

ACKNOWLEDGEMENTS
This book is dedicated to Alex, the apple of my eye.

Illustrations are acknowledged as follows: Brogdale,
National Fruit Collection, page 30 (top right); David
Burrows, page 45; Tracie Conner, page 36 (top); Richard
Edwards, page 12 (bottom); Peter Ellison, page 3; Mary
Evans Picture Library, page 28; Getty Images, cover;
Andrew Head, page 50 (top left); Heritage Images, page 9
(bottom); Joe Kingston, page 30 (top left); Museum of
English Rural Life, University of Reading, pages 13, 18
(top right), 22, 23 (both), 24, 25 (both), 26, 38, 40 (top),
42 (bottom), 44 (top); National University Library,
Prague/Bridgeman Art Library, page 6; Laura Nolte,
page 10 (top); Antonia Phillips/Broad Oak Community
Orchard, page 48; Colleen Potter, page 34 (bottom);
Private Collection, page 21; Alan Rosevear, page 42
(middle); Rob Roy, page 52 (top); Sarah Shevett, page 36
(bottom); Margaret Stewart, page 31 (bottom); James
Piers Taylor, page 52 (bottom); Keith Tomes, page 50;
Dr Alan Vaughan, page 50 (top right); Wilkin & Sons Ltd,
pages 18 (top left), and 19; John Wylie, page 32 (top).

Shire Publications is supporting the Woodland Trust, the UK's leading woodland conservation charity, by funding the dedication of trees.

CONTENTS

INTRODUCTION

ORCHARDS ARE, strictly speaking, spaces devoted to the cultivation of fruit trees, but there is much more to them than productivity. They have that irresistible quality of offering both bounty and beauty – while their fruit pleases the palate, their blossom delights the eye. Over the centuries, orchards have inspired great art and poetry and have been the setting for medieval feasts, harvest festivals and, more recently, picnics. Like forests, they are imbued with a sense of magic and mystery, encouraging tranquillity and contemplation and helping us to commune with nature in a profound way. Old orchards are also astonishingly rich habitats, offering food and shelter for over 1,800 species of wildlife, from birds and butterflies to lichens and mosses.

Covering cultural and social history, farming and agricultural practices, pastimes and traditions, flora and fauna, this book is a celebration of all the riches that orchards provide. It traces their history from their appearance in England during the Roman era to their revival over the last twenty years. Nuns and abbots, kings and queens, lords and ladies, cottagers and agricultural workers – all have enjoyed the 'beneficence' of orchards. Being the most widely grown fruit in Britain, apples have a key place in this story, but many other orchard fruit are considered, from cherries, plums and pears to hazelnuts, walnuts, quinces and the lesser-known medlar.

Today, after decades of severe decline, the ravages of foreign competition, the appearance of dwarfing rootstocks and intensely farmed bush orchards, and the rise of monoculture, traditional orchards are finally enjoying a renaissance. Regional orchard groups, community orchards and charities such as the National Trust are helping to reclaim a vital part of Britain's natural and cultural heritage. At sites throughout the country, orchards are being surveyed and restored and new ones planted, while special orchard-related events, such as Apple Day held on 21 October every year, are boosting public awareness towards the plight of local orchards. And in many of Britain's large urban centres, such as London, Birmingham and Manchester, energetic and passionate city dwellers are joining in the effort to revive orchard fruit growing. Long may it last.

Opposite:
The abundance of harvest time is brightly depicted in the September 1933 issue of *Home & Field* magazine.

5

ORIGINS AND
DEVELOPMENTS

A LTHOUGH THE CRAB APPLE, *Malus sylvestris*, is native to Britain, the orchard apple, *Malus domestica*, is not. Experts have traced it back to a single species of wild apple, *Malus sieversii*, which still grows in a remote region of Kazakhstan known as Alma-Ata (meaning – fittingly – 'Father of Apples'). As the region's nascent civilisation started to cut down forests of apples, pears and cherries in order to cultivate cereals, its people grafted the trees that produced the best fruit and planted them in orchards. From about 5,000 years ago, this type of cultivation, together with grafts and seeds, slowly spread to the Fertile Crescent and eventually into Europe.

There is, however, no evidence that orchards were cultivated in Britain before the arrival of the Romans in AD 43. During the invasion, Roman soldiers were given land as an incentive to stay and on their new plots they planted vines and orchards, as they had done back home. Writing at the same period, the poet Horace described Italy as one vast orchard; the Romans would certainly have known how to propagate and cultivate fruit trees. As they settled in Britain, they brought with them their favourite varieties of apples, cherries and grapes. Pruning hooks have been found at the Roman sites of Darenth and Hartlip in Kent, leading historians to believe that some of the county's great orchards may have first been planted during the Roman occupation. These did not remain intact for long, however. The end of Roman occupation in AD 410 opened the floodgates for attacks by Jutes, Saxons and Danes. Many of these early battles took place in Kent and obliterated the Roman orchards there.

Thanks to the arrival in England of St Augustine in AD 597, orchards were once again planted and developed, albeit mainly within the sheltered walls of monasteries. In AD 602 St Augustine built his monastery at Canterbury, establishing a model based on self-sufficiency and labour of the land, which was copied in emerging monasteries across the country. Monks and priests became expert gardeners, creating herb and vegetable gardens as well as orchards.

Evesham Abbey, which dates back to the eighth century, is said to be at the root of the Vale of Evesham's fruit-growing tradition. Records survive

Opposite:
This image from the *Opus Ruralium Commodorum* (1304–6) by Pietro de Crescenzi shows a labourer picking apples and pears from a medieval orchard. For his work on the *Opus*, which presented agricultural skills in unprecedented detail, de Crescenzi has been coined the founder of modern agronomy.

This 1873 print shows an idealised scene in an orchard in Normandy, one of the most historically important orchard regions in Europe. Labourers are celebrating the end of the apple harvest. Notice the orchard pig and geese feasting on the apples in the foreground.

Fertile soils and a sheltered climate have made the Vale of Evesham one of Britain's most favoured agricultural regions. Although orchards have declined in recent decades, the Vale is still covered in glorious blossom in the spring.

from the great monasteries at Ely near Cambridge, Christ Church in Canterbury and Battle Abbey in Sussex, which show that orchards were established at all of these sites. The first Abbot of Ely, Brithnot, is known to have planted an orchard and developed a fruit nursery there, while the first extant picture of a monastery garden comes from Christ Church and dates back to 1165: the plan shows a garden of apples and pears. The orchards at Battle Abbey in Sussex offered both useful produce and places of quiet contemplation for the monks. By the mid-eleventh century, England's monasteries and nunneries occupied about one-sixth of the land and it is fair

THE VALE OF EVESHAM

to assume that at least a few would have included an orchard of some sort. Some, such as Norwich, would have had a cherry orchard, known as a 'cherruzed'.

The term 'costermonger', or fruit seller, is a corruption of Costard, a kind of apple. Costermongers were particularly widespread in Victorian London, when they sold their produce from barrows, trays or baskets, crying their wares to attract passers-by.

The Norman Conquest of 1066 did much to increase the spread of orchards and fruit growing in England. As the Normans, who had a strong tradition of apple growing and cider making, took over the land (and the monasteries), they introduced their own farming practices, bringing with them new varieties of fruit, including the famous Costard (from which the term 'costermonger', or fruit seller, originates). Being good as an 'eater' and for cider making, it became the most widely grown apple variety in medieval England.

Production eventually reached such heights that monasteries started selling their surplus – and from the thirteenth century onwards smallholders and gardeners followed suit, taking their fruit to market. As people realised the profits that could be gained from fruit growing, market gardens became a common sight. One of the very first sites for this practice was Tower Hill, where, in the late thirteenth century, cherries were planted running down

This 1715 view of Lambeth Palace shows how much of London was surrounded by gardens, fields and orchards.

The name of this street in Clerkenwell has led experts to suggest that this spot may well have once been an orchard when monasteries and nunneries were widespread in London.

This early twentieth-century photograph of Newington illustrates just how widespread orchards were in Kent. Here, they virtually envelop the town.

towards the Thames, and sold from street stalls near St Paul's Cathedral. All around London and the rest of the country, small 'market garden orchards', often underplanted with bush fruits, vegetables or flowers for maximum productivity, started appearing.

Fruit growing was also championed by kings and queens, particularly those of French origin. Eleanor of Provence, wife of Henry III (1207–72), was keen to grow pears from her native France and had the variety 'Caillhou' grown in her gardens at Westminster and the Tower of London. At Everswell, within the park of the old royal palace of Woodstock in Oxfordshire, Henry III planted an orchard which included over a hundred pear trees in 1264. When Eleanor of Castile, wife of Henry's successor Edward I (1239–1307), developed her garden at Kings Langley in Hertfordshire, she bought grafts of the white-fleshed 'Blandurel' apple (now known as 'Calville Blanc d'Hiver') from Aquitaine. Their gardens near the

Tower of London were planted with vines and orchards of fruit trees, while at Westminster they grew nuts, quinces, peaches and cherries.

In the Tudor era, Henry VIII (1491–1547) even employed his own 'fruiterer', Richard Harris, who brought over grafts from France and the Low Countries. With these he planted a 104-acre apple and cherry orchard at Teynham in Kent, still considered by many to be the first major commercial orchard in England. From here scions were distributed to other fruit growers across the country, helping to establish other big orchards. No wonder it became known as 'the chief mother of all orchards'.

Later still, Charles I (1600–49) got his gardener John Tradescant to source new varieties of apple, cherry, medlar, quince and pear from as far away as Russia. These plants formed the basis of a vast orchard planted for Charles's French wife, Henrietta Maria, at Wimbledon Manor.

Of course whatever the royals did, the aristocracy tried to copy, and so many manorial lords started growing apples, pears and cherries as well, although it was their wives who had the task of looking after the orchards, along with the rest of the garden and the household. A distinction started to be made between the pleasure garden or orchard (*viridarium*) and the purely productive orchard (*pomerium*). The former, an intimate and often enclosed space featuring fruit trees, fragrant flowers and herbs, a lawn dotted with small flowers, and often a fountain and turf bench, was designed to delight the senses and inspire romance. The latter would have been much larger and planted in a regimented fashion, either in wide rows or following the classic quincunx formation (four trees in a square and one in the centre, like the 'five' on a dice).

Kent, the Garden of England, has for centuries been known for its cherry orchards – such as these in Newington.

Cherry Orchards at Newington.

Thornbury Castle in Gloucestershire, for example, featured ' a goodly orchard full of young grafftes well laden with frute, many roses and other pleasures'.

By 1600 most farmhouses, manors, vicarages and castles would have been self-sufficient in fruit. The growing number and availability of books, thanks to advances in printing since its development by Gutenberg in the fifteenth century, helped spread the word about fruit growing and orchards. In 1618 William Lawson published *A New Orchard and Garden (or The best way for Planting, Grafting, and to make any ground good, for a rich Orchard)*, which became a source of inspiration for manor and farmhouse gardeners. In it Lawson describes how a well-designed orchard might look: designed with ornamental knots, topiary, bee hives and mounts to look

One of the first great plant hunters, botanists and garden designers, John Tradescant the Elder (c. 1570– 1638) created gardens, including orchards, for the rich and famous, such as Sir Robert Cecil and King Charles I.

More commonly cultivated in the medieval era, the medlar deserves a place in the modern orchard. The fruits need to be 'bletted', a process that involves leaving them to sweeten and almost rot after picking.

down from, it 'makes all our senses swimme in pleasure and that with infinite variety, joined with no less commodity'. Other practical books, concerned mainly with propagation and planting, made a strong impact too, including Leonard Mascall's *Booke of Arte and Maner, howe to plant and graffe all sorts of trees* (1590), Anthony Fitzherbert's *Book of Husbandry* (1525) and Ralph Austen's *A Treatise of Fruit Trees* (1653), in which the author went as far as stating that it should be compulsory to plant orchards.

A figure with more influence than anyone else on the growth of orchards in the seventeenth century was Lord Scudamore (1601–71). During his time as Charles I's ambassador at the court of Louis XIII in France, he discovered a new apple, which he named 'Redstreak', and learnt much about French orcharding and cidermaking. On his return to England, he applied his new knowledge and started making the very best and strongest cider Britons had ever drunk. The Redstreak quickly became an extremely profitable crop, a

The Redstreak was the finest and most expensive cider apple of seventeenth-century England.

13

fact which led farmers and landowners to plant new orchards on pasture land and arable fields. Some landowners even forced their tenants to do the same – a point made by James Russell in his book *Man-made Eden: Historic Orchards in Somerset and Gloucestershire*:

> In such ignominious deals was borne what we now call the traditional orchard with standard trees planted in small (two-acre) fields in such a way that the land could be used for the raising of livestock or growth of crops ... For many cottagers the apple crop was by far the biggest source of income. The effect was to create a highly visible landscape of orchards.

Fruit growing proved a godsend for farmers and smallholders in the midst of an agricultural slump during the mid- to late seventeenth century. Along with cider varieties, table (or culinary) apples became increasingly popular and profitable, with apples and other fruits being more commonly eaten raw – a practice which was virtually unheard of in the medieval era (apart from the eating of raw cherries) – or cooked in delicious pies and puddings. By the end of the seventeenth century, orchards would have been a common sight in Kent, Herefordshire, Somerset, Gloucestershire and Worcestershire. Existing orchard areas, such as those in Kent and London, expanded rapidly while at the same time developments in water transport helped larger quantities of fruit to reach market and enabled new orchard sites to develop.

The Restoration of the Monarchy in 1660 saw an end to decades of upheaval and heralded the start of a peaceful and, indeed, fruitful era. The nation's new quest for scientific knowledge, embodied by the foundation of the Royal Society in 1660, certainly had an impact on fruit production. At the time, many fruit growers and farmers had only a vague idea which varieties they were growing; some of them were even known under two or more names, depending on where they were grown. Thanks to the introduction of pomonas – those beautifully illustrated and detailed fruit 'catalogues' – growers were increasingly able to identify and learn about apples, pears and other fruit. The famous gardener and writer John Evelyn wrote one of the very first pomonas as an appendix to the second edition of his great work, *Sylva, or a Discourse of Forest Trees* (1670). The content was based on discussions with his colleagues at the Royal Society. London-based garden designer and writer Batty Langley wrote his *Pomona, or the Fruit Garden Illustrated* in 1729. Its large black-and-white detailed prints paved the way for the colourful pomonas of the nineteenth century and beyond, all beautifully illustrated with intricate botanical art.

New scientific endeavours eventually led to the introduction of controlled breeding methods, particularly those developed by the

Herefordshire-based horticulturalist Thomas Andrew Knight (1759–1838), who was the first to produce reliable varieties through cross-pollination.

The growing interest in gardening and all things horticultural encouraged the growth of private orchards throughout the country during the eighteenth century. Furthermore, the development of the canal network in the latter part of the century made the establishment of new orchards a commercial possibility. The opening of the Staffordshire and Worcestershire Canal in 1772 certainly fuelled the expansion of Worcestershire's orchards, which further expanded in the nineteenth century with the arrival of the railways. Canals were also responsible for helping to boost the cider industry and, with it, the growth of cider apple orchards.

And yet, despite this general growth, commercial fruit growing actually experienced a decline in the mid- to late eighteenth century. Increased profits gained from corn and livestock (both from their meat and milk) altered farmers' attitudes to growing fruit, which in turn led to poor or at least reduced orchard management. This, coupled with the spread of fruit tree disease, particularly canker, eventually caused the demise of many old fruit varieties, including the famous Redstreak. Moreover, by the end of the eighteenth century cider drinking was being overtaken in popularity by imported wine, so it is surprising that orchards survived at all. But survive they did, thanks to the positive and far-reaching impacts of the Industrial Revolution and the verve of the apple-worshipping Victorians.

This print, entitled 'Apple Harvesting', featured in an 1873 edition of *The Illustrated London News*. In the late Victorian era, orchards and especially apples enjoyed a renaissance.

SKETCHES AT THE APPLE CONGRESS AT CHISWICK.

HEYDAY AND DECLINE

HAD IT NOT been for the Industrial Revolution, a good many of Britain's orchards would no doubt have disappeared during the nineteenth century. The emergence and growth of the railway network and the huge rise in population during this era increased the demand for and availability of food, including fruit. As a result, and despite the desperate condition of some of Britain's orchards, the number of orchards actually rose during the nineteenth century, particularly in the later decades. Kent, for instance, saw its fruit-growing acreage rise from 10,000 in 1873 to 25,000 in 1898. While established orchard areas such as Kent and Somerset grew, new ones also appeared. In Worcestershire, the local Pershore plum became a speciality. Cambridgeshire focused on the delicious Cambridge Gage. Lancashire, Cheshire, Nottinghamshire and Cornwall all developed orchard hotspots. By the end of the nineteenth century, every county had its orchards.

The establishment of the Midland Railway's Oxford, Worcester and Wolverhampton line in 1852 led to the planting of new orchards in Herefordshire. From here apples could be taken by train to the large urban markets in the Midlands and London. A few large orchards ran their own trains, and Lord Sudeley's 1,000-acre Toddington Orchard Company in Gloucestershire even had its own terminus. By the early decades of the twentieth century, some railway companies had special fruit-handling premises and fleets of lorries collected fruit from orchards within reach of stations.

Because, thanks to the Empire's trading system, sugar was cheaper in Britain than anywhere else in the nineteenth century, a successful jamming industry developed. Realising the value of using plums as an alternative to more expensive strawberries in their preserves, jam makers, such as the John Chivers Company established in 1873, helped boost plum production and keep orchards going. Wilkin & Sons of Tiptree, another big jam producer, bought fruit, such as the Cambridge Gage, from Essex and Cambridgeshire. It still produces preserves today using fruit farmed from 1,000 acres near the village of Tiptree in Essex.

Opposite: This print published in *The Illustrated London News* features humorous sketches inspired by the 1883 National Apple Congress. Notice some of the descriptive apple names, such as Catshead, Lemon Pippin and Lady's Finger.

Above:
Wilkin & Sons was established in Tiptree, Essex, in 1885 and famously made preserves using a variety of fruit, as this poster displays. The jamming industry played a key part in the development of orchards during the late nineteenth century.

Right: *Returning from the Orchard* (1907), an oil painting by the Cornish painter Harold Harvey (1874–1941).

Founded in 1804, the Horticultural Society (which became the Royal Horticultural Society in 1861) was particularly helpful in encouraging fruit growing and disseminating practical and scientific knowledge both to commercial growers and the wider public. It ran fruit trials, encouraged the breeding of new varieties, published practical information on fruit production and even built up its own fruit collection at its garden in Chiswick. Between 1828 and 1830 it produced a *Pomological Magazine*, featuring intricate illustrations of different fruit varieties cultivated in Britain, accompanied by detailed descriptions.

Thanks in part to the work of the Horticultural Society the nineteenth century saw a rise in the production of exquisitely illustrated pomonas. Published by George Brookshaw in 1812, the great *Pomona Britannica, or a Collection of the Most Esteemed Fruits at Present Cultivated in this Country* featured 256 species of fifteen kinds of fruit. Perhaps even more astonishing was the *Pomona Herefordiensis*, published in 1811 by Thomas Andrew Knight. It has been described as a masterpiece, and rightly so. Each of the highly detailed illustrations (some are so realistic they even show leaf and fruit damage) is hand-coloured, making every copy unique. Had it not been for one enterprising local society – the Woolhope Naturalists' Field Club – this book might never have come into being. Worried about the state of Herefordshire's cider orchards, the society decided to carry out a survey of the county's orchards. The fruit expert Dr Robert Hogg led the survey and the results of his research were published in the pomona. His work was so comprehensive that Hogg subsequently became known as the 'father of British pomology'.

Eventually all this interest in fruit, and particularly apples, led to the establishment of the British Pomological Society in 1854, while the increasingly scientific approach to fruit growing resulted in the introduction of new varieties. Research was undertaken, for instance, to enable the production of a new variety of plum whose blossom would be more resistant to frost: plum trees flower earlier than other fruiting trees and are therefore more at risk of frost damage. Specialist breeders, such as Thomas Laxton of Buckingham, developed many new varieties. He and his

Opposite top right: This fruit picker for Wilkin & Sons is busy harvesting cherries to be used in the company's preserves.

Below: This hand-coloured print from the exquisite *Pomona Herefordiensis* depicts the Blenheim Orange, a dual-purpose apple with a delicious nutty flavour.

Cox's Orange Pippin was introduced in the 1850s and, since its commercial production in the 1860s, has been the most popular apple grown in Britain.

grandsons after him produced some of our most popular and tasty apples (Lord Lambourne, Laxton's Fortune and Laxton's Superb) as well as plums (Early Laxton and Laxton's Supreme), pears and other soft fruits such as strawberries and raspberries. The RHS awarded medals to the best new varieties of fruit, a fact which must have fuelled growers' enthusiasm and interest. In about 1835, retired brewer Richard Cox grew the very first Cox's Orange Pippin, perhaps the most popular apple ever to be raised in Britain. It won an RHS Gold Medal.

Apple imports from abroad – particularly France and the United States, but also Canada, New Zealand and Australia – started to threaten British orchards from the late 1870s onwards. Rather than give in, though, the British became passionate about their 'national fruit'. Apples – their taste, appearance, smell, cooking potential – became a topic of serious and heated debate. The French might have their fine wines, but the British had their apples and started discussing particular varieties as if they were an expensive claret. The wealthy started reintroducing apple trees into their private gardens, creating 'artistic orchards' inspired by the medieval and Tudor eras. At the same time, the eternal beauty of orchards inspired many late nineteenth-century British artists – such as Sir George Clausen and Henry Herbert La Thangue – to produce wonderfully lyrical images of orchards.

Soon a national campaign to save British orchards was under way, culminating in the National Apple Congress of 1883 held at the Great Vinery in the RHS gardens at Chiswick. The show was so popular that it had to stay open an extra week to meet demand. 'Never before had so many varieties been brought together in one place and probably never will again,' wrote apple expert Joan Morgan in *The New Book of Apples*.

For the show, a committee of fifty experts was convened: they identified a total of 1,545 different varieties from the apples exhibited and ultimately produced a list of the top best dessert and culinary apples, which included Cox's Orange Pippin and Bramley's Seedling. The most popular apples on this list eventually became the staples of Britain's apple orchards. In fact, Cox's Orange Pippin became so popular that experts estimate that about half of all the apple trees planted in Britain in the inter-war years were of this variety.

There is an irony here: while the National Apple Congress and national interest in apples encouraged an appreciation of their varying tastes, textures and appearances, the final compilation of these 'best apples' actually led to a reduction in the number of different apples grown commercially. The competition from abroad helped reinforce this trend, by making it almost compulsory for apple growers to concentrate on a small number of reliable (and also long-lived) varieties, rather than focusing on taste and locality as a priority. As we shall see, this development eventually led to the rise in monoculture which has blighted much of Britain's farming industry. As a result of foreign competition, most of the small market gardens were eventually swept away, unable to compete with bigger commercial growers and their economies of scale.

Developments in 'fruit technology' continued unhindered though, probably boosted by all this foreign competition. In 1894 Woburn Experimental Fruit Farm was established; it was the first centre ever to focus on fruit experimentation. In 1903, the Fruit Research Station was founded at Long Ashton in Somerset, followed in 1913 by the now world-famous East Malling Research Station in Kent. It was here that eminent pomologist Ronald Hatton worked on the testing and standardisation of apple rootstocks, which became known as the 'Malling series'. And in 1922 nurseryman and fruit expert Edward Bunyard set up the Commercial Fruit Trials at RHS Wisley in order to establish and select the most commercially viable fruit varieties. This in turn led to the establishment of the National Fruit Trials at

Rural orchards inspired many nineteenth- and early twentieth-century artists, including Monet, Van Gogh, Pissarro and other lesser-known painters such as John McDougal, who painted *In a Gloucestershire Orchard* (1924).

Brogdale in Kent. The site is now home to the National Fruit Collection – one of the world's great 'mother orchards', home to over 3,500 named varieties of fruit. It has been described as a living museum: a gene bank for later generations, acting as a vital source of grafting material for the propagation of old and rare varieties.

The size of the rootstock is vital in controlling the growth and size of a fruit tree. The emergence of semi-dwarfing rootstocks in the early twentieth century inevitably led to changes in the look of commercial orchards. Some old orchards were even grubbed up to make way for these new 'bush orchards'. Planted in tight, ordered rows, the smaller trees produced fruit much earlier than their larger cousins. They also required less pruning and enjoyed a higher yield. The only drawback, it seemed, was that they had a shorter lifespan – about twenty years, rather than fifty

This 1954 photograph shows a Bramley apple orchard in Kent being sprayed with arsenic of lead to protect the trees against codling moth. No measures were too great to safeguard the crop from this pest.

22

years or more. By the 1970s, growers moved to even smaller dwarfing trees, which reached about 2 metres in height when mature. Being small, they were particularly easy to harvest, yielded an inordinate number of fruit compared to their actual size, and bore fruit when they were only three or four years old, rather than eight to ten years for a standard tree. But there was a downside to all this: animals were unable to graze under such small, tightly packed trees and pesticides had to be used to control the grass and weeds surrounding them.

An avenue of oil-filled 'smoke bombs' in an Evesham orchard, 1939. At the first sign of frost, the farmer would light the bombs; the warm smoke emitted by the oil was enough to keep the frost away from the trees.

The fertiliser sulphate of ammonia is scattered by hand on a Morello cherry orchard at Wested Farm, Crockenhill, Kent, in 1949. Note the old stump with the new graftings.

Along with the rest of the agricultural world, commercial fruit tree growers became heavily reliant on chemicals. Insecticides and fungicides became commonplace and new spray technologies were developed to help control pests and diseases, such as mildew, scab, codling moths and aphids. Arsenic of lead was a popular choice for killing off codling moths' eggs. Astonishingly, special protective suits were only enforced by the middle of the century by The Summary of Agriculture (Poisonous Substances) Regulation of 1953. Night-time spraying was favoured by some growers, who believed that the air was more still then. It also meant that other essential work could be carried out during the day. Huge and powerful floodlights had to be carried into the orchards to illuminate the trees and sprayers.

Frost damage was a major concern too and, with the help of new technologies, some growers went to great lengths to protect their trees. Hot

Giant 'hot air blowers' were used for frost protection. This 1948 photograph shows a blower being started up at Jacksbridge Farm, Surrey. Conveniently mounted on a trailer, the machine was driven around the orchard directing warm air towards the trees.

air heaters and 'smoke bombs' might seem incongruous in an orchard, but they were successfully used to keep trees just above freezing. In the 1930s Mr Harrington, an amateur fruit-grower from Bedford, designed his 'Harrington Orchard Heaters'. These tin canisters were filled with crude oil and lit when the temperature fell. In the 1940s, vast hot air blowers were introduced. Cylinders filled with propane gas were placed on trailers and pulled by tractors throughout the orchards, directing warm air through the trees. According to one witness, the noise was 'rather tiresome to nearby sleepers – but surely this is nothing to the saving of thousands of bushels of fruit.'

This 1952 photograph shows Mr L.M. Adam from Uphill Fruit Farm, Edenbridge, Kent, sizing recently cropped apples on a special gauge, prior to packing.

This stand at a 1950s agricultural show displays specimen grafts. It also promotes orchard improvement competitions and orchard pruning classes – steps designed to encourage good orchard management practice.

The Ministry of Food sponsored new grading, packing and storing facilities throughout the country in order to 'save Britain dollars' and resist the threat of American imports. This 1949 photograph shows apples being graded, sorted, weighed and packed by women using a new conveyor belt system.

All sorts of other contraptions were introduced to boost productivity and efficiency. There were, for instance, machines that could plant up to 20,000 rootstocks per day. The arts of picking, wrapping and storing became more complex and sophisticated, as apple graders, wrapping machines and cutting-edge storage facilities were developed. In the 1950s, apple harvesting, pruning and grafting demonstrations also became available. East Malling conducted fruit storage trials and the first National Apple Packing Contest was held at the East Kent Fruit Show in November 1950.

This was all part of a post-Second World War drive to improve the nation's interest in and knowledge of fruit growing, but it did little to stem the tide of destruction. While the early decades of the twentieth century had been relatively good for orchards – their total acreage rising from about 250,000 in 1910 to 273,000 in 1950 – the second half of the century witnessed a steady and severe decline. The Second World War hit fruit growers particularly hard. Ironically, the wartime 'Grow your Own'

campaign led to the grubbing up of orchards in favour of vegetable production. After the war, many old orchards were not considered profitable enough and were replaced with other more lucrative crops.

The growth of towns and cities, as well as the increasing numbers of roads and infrastructures, also led to the loss of orchards. A notable example was the development of Heathrow Airport, which swept away most of the Thames Valley orchards. Tell-tale signs of old orchards appear in cities, towns and villages across the country, where street names can be found bearing the name 'Orchard'.

When Britain joined the European Economic Community (EEC) in 1973, fruit growers faced fierce competition from other member countries, particularly France and Holland. France had its famous Golden Delicious, which with its impeccable looks and long shelf-life became the apple of choice for many European stores. What's more, the French and Dutch fruit industries were organised in large co-operatives, which gave them clout in the market. British growers responded to this threat by promoting their own 'unique selling points', namely their own indigenous apples: the Cox and the Bramley. As James Russell writes in *Man-made Eden*:

> With few exceptions, any orchard that wanted to stay in business needed to grow the 'English' varieties – Cox's Orange Pippin and Bramley – and to use all available resources, chemical, mechanical, to maximise yields and ensure fruit productivity.

Over recent decades, UK farmers have joined forces into large co-operatives, enabling them to share up-to-the-minute machinery and exchange expertise. But there are certain things that they just cannot defeat – particularly cheap imports. The fact that major British cider producers can buy cheap apple concentrate from abroad has inevitably meant the decline in the number of cider orchards in the UK.

Yet another blow came in 1991 with the introduction of the Apple Orchard Grubbing Up Scheme, which saw farmers being offered £4,600 per hectare to dig up apple orchards (with the exception of cider orchards) – the aim being to stop the overproduction of apples across the EEC.

All these factors led to the near-demise of the UK's orchard industry. While in 1970 there were 62,000 hectares of orchards in the country, by 1997 there were just 22,400. Kent has lost 85 per cent of its orchards in the last fifty years; Somerset 50 per cent. Today, Britain imports an astounding 75 per cent of its apples.

Thankfully, and as we shall see in the final chapter, over the last two decades orchards have become the focus of much positive attention, with more and more people realising their long-term significance.

FLORA AND FAUNA

Featuring facts and anecdotes, the first part of this chapter provides a brief introduction to the astonishing diversity of Britain's orchard fruits. The second part offers an insight into the rich habitats harboured by old-fashioned orchards.

The limited range of apples, pears, plums and cherries available in our supermarkets belies their amazing diversity. There are actually over 2,300 varieties of dessert and cooking apples growing in the United Kingdom, as well as hundreds of different cider apples.

Many varieties are the product of specific localities, being particularly suited to their site's soil and weather. Often, their names bear testament to their origins. The Blenheim Orange, for instance, was first grown by a tailor named George Kempster in the 1740s near Blenheim Palace in Oxfordshire. The local calcareous soil is said to be ideal for this apple tree, whose large fruit features a crumbly texture and a lovely nutty flavour and can be used both for eating and cooking. In Cornwall, cherries known as Burcombes and Birchenhayes were named after their place of origin, a phenomenon which is typical of the rest of the country.

Other names are wonderfully evocative, including Burr Knot, so called because it bears knots at the base of branches which root if planted; Catshead, which when viewed from a certain angle resembles its name; and Lemon Pippin, which is yellow, shaped like a lemon and sometimes smells slightly lemony as well. The same can be said of Ananas Reinette, an unusual variety whose strong pineapple smell (*ananas* means 'pineapple' in French) is matched by a similar flavour. Other names are more humorous, such as the cider apples Slack ma Girdle and Bastard Rough Coat!

Pear varieties also are abundant, with over 3,000 recorded worldwide and about 550 varieties grown in the United Kingdom. Gloucester is home to over one hundred different types of perry pear, including the wonderfully named Merrylegs, Drunkers and Devildrink, which more than hint at their inebriating effects. While few apple orchards live to be over a hundred years old, pear and cherry orchards can reach a much riper age.

Opposite: Mistletoe grows on a variety of trees, including poplars, willows and hawthorns, but its favoured host is the apple tree.

Above: Pear trees can live for three hundred years or more, looking as majestic as ancient oaks in the landscape.

Above right: Ananas Reinette has an unusual pineapple flavour and scent.

The perry pear orchard on the outskirts of Brockworth near Gloucester, saved from development in 2008, has trees that are said to be three hundred years old. Like ancient oak trees, these 'monuments in the landscape' are part of Britain's horticultural heritage. Silent survivors in an ever-changing landscape, they deserve to be preserved.

Before the twentieth century, cherries were grown in such quantities – particularly in Kent – that they weren't just sold fresh, but were also turned into cherry brandy, wine and even ale. The West Country, especially Devon, was once famous for a cherry known as the 'mazzard', said to have been introduced by the Huguenots in the eighteenth century. Buckinghamshire was famous for its orchards of jet-black 'Prestwood Black' cherries, known locally known as 'Chuggies'.

Similarly there are many local variations of plums. The villages of Weston Turville and Totternhoe near Aylesbury were known for a black plum known as the 'Aylesbury Prune'. Other areas had their own specialities, such as Pershore Purple, Shropshire Prune and Warwickshire Drooper, which as its name suggests has an attractive weeping habit. It produces an abundance of succulent yellow fruits, which are equally flavoursome whether eaten raw or cooked. The area surrounding Kendal in Cumbria was once a thriving damson-producing region. Some historians have argued that during the nineteenth century the sharp-tasting damson

A Kent cherry orchard grazed by sheep. Cherry trees can reach incredible heights – up to 25 metres – making their fruit particularly challenging to harvest.

was particularly popular with inhabitants of northern industrial towns because their palates had been dulled by the constant effects of factory fumes and smoke.

Orchards have also been home to more unusual fruits, such as medlars and quinces, as well as a variety of nuts, including walnuts and hazelnuts. Popular in the Middle Ages, medlars are sadly overlooked nowadays, perhaps because they produce an unpromising-looking, hard fruit. After picking, medlars need to be left to soften for at least two weeks – a process known as 'bletting'. Quinces, although fairly common in Southern Europe, are sadly quite rare in Britain nowadays. Although the fruit cannot be eaten raw, it more than makes up for this in its exquisitely perfumed taste when cooked as jelly or marmalade, in tarts, or as a paste which is delicious eaten with cheese.

Introduced in about 1830, the Kentish cobnut is a variety of cultivated hazelnut. During the Victorian era its cultivation became widespread in this county, and it is now enjoying a revival thanks to the Kentish Cobnuts Association.

Hazelnuts and walnuts were once commonly found in orchards. While walnuts were consumed fresh or turned into oil, their wood was also harvested and so were the walnut shells, which made a long-lasting black dye, often used as a hair dye. Orchards of grand houses were sometimes reached through a nuttery or nut alley, such as the one at Sissinghurst in Kent. In the eighteenth and nineteenth centuries, hazelnuts were sometimes planted

KENTISH COBNUTS

together with hops, apple and cherry trees. Once the fruit trees had matured and needed more room, the hops and the hazelnuts were grubbed up. The area around Maidstone in Kent has long been associated with the Kentish Cob, a variety of hazelnut. By 1913, Kentish Cob orchards, known as 'plats', covered an area of over 7,000 acres in the region.

Beyond their obvious aim of producing fruit, old orchards are incredibly rich micro-

In the spring, blossoming orchards are a hotspot for bees and other pollinating insects.

The Lesser Spotted Woodpecker is Britain's smallest and rarest woodpecker and thrives in old orchards. It nests in decaying trees and feeds off beetles that harbour in the dead wood.

habitats, providing a home to a diverse range of flora and fauna. Sue Clifford wrote in the *Common Ground Book of Orchards*: 'Neither woodland, grassland, hedgerow or wood pasture, orchards rarely feature in habitat surveys. Yet the wonder of these places stems from the fact that they can be all these habitats at once.' Although many have disappeared, the old orchards that have survived have thankfully escaped the onslaught of insecticides and fertilisers used on farmland and commercial orchards, and have therefore become valuable havens for a rich variety of species.

Small birds, such as nuthatches, treecreepers, tree sparrows, little owls and tits, nest or feed amongst the wood, while spiders, beetles, ladybirds and other insects live, nest or hibernate in the decaying wood of the older trees. The larvae of the Noble Chafer Beetle are particularly attracted to old apple, plum and cherry trees. Because of the loss of old orchards in the past hundred years, the Noble Chafer has become increasingly rare; it is now a Biodiversity Action Plan species and has been classed as 'vulnerable'.

Some birds are particularly associated with orchards, relying heavily on them for their continued livelihood. The Lesser Spotted Woodpecker feeds on larvae, spiders and wood-boring insects. It is an elusive creature, which you are more likely to spot in winter and early spring, before leaves emerge on the trees. Another member of the woodpecker family, the Wryneck nests in the cavities of old orchard trees and feasts on ants and other insects. Although now rare, it can still be spotted in the south-east of England. With its powerful beak, the discreet Hawfinch is an expert at cracking open cherry stones. It builds a small nest in amongst the branches of fruit trees, much like the Bullfinch, which is often seen as the scourge of the fruit grower, as it has a fondness for devouring the buds of orchard trees.

To protect their crop from such 'pests', orchardists sometimes planted extra 'sacrificial' trees as well as hedgerows around the orchard, featuring a mixture of wild and cultivated fruit trees, in the hope that these would reduce the damage done to the main trees. Rather than relying on chemical solutions, there is evidence to suggest that naturally managed orchards are

Below: The Wryneck is best spotted in orchards in the south-east of England during August and September.

Bottom: The bud-devouring Bullfinch was once treated as an orchard pest. Its numbers have declined, making this beautiful bird less of a nuisance to the fruit-grower.

A rare migrant to Britain, the Camberwell Beauty likes to feed off ripe orchard fruit.

During the winter, Mistle Thrushes feast on the white flesh of mistletoe berries, after which they clean their beaks on the branches of the apple tree – a process which helps the mistletoe reproduce and spread throughout the orchard.

Among other plants, the common Red Admiral likes to feed off apple blossom in spring and decaying fruit in the autumn.

better in the long run for combating pests and diseases. Sue Clifford wrote in the *Common Ground Book of Orchards*:

> An insect-rich orchard comes equipped with nature's own pesticide squad – a complex array of natural predators. Recent research shows that this natural armoury can, in the long term, keep pest species at bay much more effectively than any chemical spray ever can.

In the spring, honeybees, bumblebees and wasps help pollinate the trees and in the past, beehives were indeed a common feature in old orchards. Those that were walled sometimes feature beeholes in which bee skeps would have been placed. Sadly, commercial orchards nowadays rent out hives when needed for pollination, a phenomenon known as 'migratory beekeeping'.

In the winter, the leafless trees are 'decorated' with mistletoe, whose white berries provide valuable food for Mistle Thrushes and other birds. At the same time, windfalls attract a range of wildlife, such

as butterflies (including the rare Camberwell Beauty and masses of Red Admirals and Commas), moths (including the Yellow Underwing), hedgehogs and badgers. Fieldfare and Redwing are a common sight in the colder months, when whole flocks gather in orchards to feast on the fruit. The rotting fruit also acts as a source of nutrients for toadstools and other fungi.

This yearly process of death and rebirth creates a virtuous cycle – a web of interdependence between plants and animals. And therein lies the beauty of old orchards. Even neglected or apparently unnecessary features can harbour valuable plants

The easily spotted Yellow Underwing is one of Britain's most common moths and is abundant throughout the country.

Fieldfare and Redwing are often found in apple orchards during the winter months, when they congregate in large groups to eat the fallen fruit.

Keeping hens in an orchard is an age-old tradition. The birds keep insects and other pests down, they help weed the soil, and their droppings provide nutrients.

Traditional orchards often host domesticated animals, such as sheep, hens, cattle, pigs and geese. While sheep keep the grass short, their dung adds important nutrients to the soil.

and animals. Old walls are ideal homes for spiders and other crevice-living insects, as well as ivy, a source of winter nectar for insects. A pile of old wood is the perfect habitat for hedgehogs, while a decaying tree stump can provide protection and food for many insects. Meanwhile, grasses, such as Red Fescue, Crested Dog's Tail and Cocksfoot, as well as wildflowers, including Bird's Foot Trefoil, Field Scabious, Wood Anemone and the Common Spotted Orchid, can be found growing in the undisturbed soil under the trees, attracting yet more spiders, moths, butterflies and other insects.

As well as reaping the rewards of wild creatures such as birds and bees, fruit growers have also long seen the benefit of introducing animals into the orchard. For centuries sheep or cattle were employed to keep the orchard grass down, but also to provide manure for the trees. Meanwhile, the trees provided shelter for the animals, particularly during the hot summer months. A. Major, author of *Cherries in the Rise: Cherry Cultivation in Kent*, remembers that it was common practice to 'stock twelve sheep to the acre in summer and six in winter'. He recalls, during harvest time, having 'to keep a sharp eye open on chips full of picked cherries otherwise the sheep would help themselves'. Pigs, goats, geese and hens were also frequently used.

Biodiversity is enhanced if the orchard features trees of different ages and of different species, something which was quite widespread before the rise of monoculture and the appearance of dwarfing rootstocks. The rural traveller William Cobbett commented on this fact when describing the orchards between Maidstone and Mereworth in *Rural Rises* (1820):

Entitled 'The Mistletoe Gatherer', this Victorian print is a nostalgic depiction of a wonderful Christmas tradition: that of collecting mistletoe for decorating the home and, of course, for the mistletoe kiss.

> This is what people of Kent call the Garden of England. It is a district of meadows, hop gardens and orchards of apples, pears, cherries and filberts … The culture is sometimes mixed; that is to say, apple trees and cherry trees or filbert trees and hops in the same ground.

This practice sadly ended in the middle of the twentieth century. That some plants and animals rely on orchards for their survival is underlined by the fact that apple orchards now harbour 80 per cent of all the mistletoe grown in the UK. And so, without old orchards, one of the most charming traditions of the Christmas season could be lost, along with many other well-loved rituals and pastimes, as we shall see in the next chapter.

PASTIMES AND PRACTICES

L IKE ALL PRODUCTIVE PLOTS, orchards are subject to many annual practices, the most important and satisfying of which is probably the harvest. Until at least the mid-twentieth century, harvesting was a community effort, as one resident from Helsby in Cheshire recalls in *Orchards of Cheshire*:

> All the local women were employed for the fruit harvest and their baskets were marked with a piece of slate with their mark or name on it. Any picker with two or three girls in the family who were old enough to help gained handsomely, as they could pick three or four times as much. The children's picking was counted towards the mother's work.

In *Cherries in the Rise: Cherry Cultivation in Kent*, author A. Major writes about picking cherries in the 1940s to 1960s:

> We who picked these orchards were all locals. We lived at home and went to the orchards in the evenings after work, at weekends or as part of a holiday from our usual job to earn extra money. We were paid at the end of each week until the cherry season was finished. Then we were finished until the next cherry season, unless of course, we went on to apple and pear picking.

Cherry picking was known in certain areas as 'cherrying'. Women, who were generally considered faster pickers than men, harvested in small groups, about three per tree. Before the appearance of dwarfing rootstocks and smaller trees, ladders were an essential part of the harvesting process. Each gang of cherry pickers had a male ladder mover or 'setter'. It was his duty to make sure that the tall ladders were safely set on the tree. This was quite a responsibility, as cherry trees can reach 25 metres in height and have many weak branches. The setter would often secure the ladder against the tree twice, so that if the higher setting let go there was an extra 'safety net' underneath. Given the responsibility of this task, pickers would often complain if their usual setter was replaced by someone else. During the

Opposite:
Picking cherries at Stockbury, near Sittingbourne, Kent in 1952. Note the younger boys 'footing' the ladders for extra safety.

This woman is harvesting a crop of Cox's Orange Pippins at Norton Fruit Farm, near Yeovil.

Victorian and Edwardian eras, women's attire made the possibility of falling out of a tree even more real: their full-length skirts and dresses certainly didn't help with balance or ease of movement.

Pickers collected the cherries – with stalks, or 'strigs', attached, otherwise the fruit could get damaged or go bad – into a special basket known as a 'kibsy' or 'kipsy'. This was tied securely around the waist of the picker and featured a flat side that would rest against the

This print, published in the *The Illustrated London News* in 1886, shows labourers – young and old – harvesting apples.

back. Pickers could also use a long, often homemade, hook to pull faraway branches towards them.

In some orchards the fruit was sent straight to market; in others, locals would visit during harvest time to buy a pound or so of the freshly picked fruit. After the harvest, the smaller, unripe cherries were left on the trees. These were known as 'scrumps' and were often picked at the end of the cherry season. Pickers would then go 'scrumping' throughout the entire orchard and were usually paid by the hour, rather than according to the quantity of cherries picked.

Even while they were picking fruit, Victorian and Edwardian women wore long skirts and dresses, increasing the likelihood of accidents occurring while using ladders.

Of course harvesting practices varied depending on the type of orchard fruit. In cider orchards, pickers used long harvest poles to knock down the fruit. The main concern was getting the fruit out of the trees rather than gathering perfect specimens. In Hereford, the fruit was heaped into straw-covered piles and left to 'sweat' for two to three weeks. The apples would lose

Fruit picking was a community event a hundred years ago, as this Edwardian postcard shows.

POPULAR SONG ILLUSTRATED. "I WANT YER MA HONEY"

some of their moisture content and become sweeter in the process. In other counties, including Devon and Somerset, the apples were spread on the upper floor of the cider mill for the same process to take place. Fruit that was destined for jam-making was also part-processed on site, as was the case in some plum orchards, where the fruit was actually pulped at the farm and stored in barrels in the orchard before being taken to the jam-makers.

A couple of scrumpers are about to get their come-uppance! In traditional cherry orchards, 'scrumping' involved picking the last remaining fruit off the trees after the main harvest had taken place.

Old cider wagons can still be seen at Perry's Cider, in Dowlish Wake, Somerset. The site also features a small yet fascinating cider museum.

Pulped plums in barrels are kept in the orchard of Mr Jack Lee of Crockenhill, Kent, 1947, awaiting collection from the jam makers. The fruit is stored in the shade of the trees to stop the heat of the sun from exploding the barrels.

An early twentieth-century postcard entitled 'Spring Cleaning in the Orchard'. Orchard bonfires – whether in the summer or autumn – were an easy way to get rid of unwanted, dead or diseased wood.

Harvesting is of course the most obvious orchard practice, but there were many activities. Winter was the time for pruning, after which an orchard bonfire would be lit to destroy all the clippings. In the spring, the soil might be rotavated to allow for crops to be planted in between the trees. In early summer, some trees were thinned – a process which ensured a better size and quality of fruit and reduced the risk of broken branches. In the summer, when the fruit started to ripen, a number of scaring tactics were used to protect the crops against birds. One method, which survived until the mid-twentieth century, involved sending a lad around the orchard to make as much noise as possible, using devices such as rattles and clappers. Boys were also employed to fly bird-shaped kites above the orchard.

Springtime in this orchard involved preparing the land for the planting of crops alongside the fruit trees.

This 1960s photo shows a small bunch of apples before thinning. Bunches all over the tree were reduced to a single fruit, a process which helped to produce better-tasting and larger apples.

In the twentieth century some orchards were transformed into impromptu or permanent tea gardens, such as the Orchard Tea Gardens at Bossington in Somerset. Note how the tables have been specially designed to wrap around the tree trunks.

Sometimes metal objects connected by a wire or rope were hung from tree branches: every time someone gave the rope a tug, the objects would clang together. Some orchard owners even resorted to firing a gun at regular intervals. In the autumn, poachers could also be a serious problem. This was such a concern to orchardists in the Swanley area of Kent that in 1963 they went as far as erecting wire fences and hiring guard dogs to patrol the orchards at night.

As well as being places of hard labour, orchards have long been associated with celebrations and relaxation. For many of us nowadays, they represent a kind of rural idyll: a place in which to enjoy nature in all its beauty and bounty. This was certainly the case for Muriel Berry, who remembers playing in her local orchard as a young girl in the mid-twentieth century, as quoted in *Orchards of Cheshire*:

In the drowsy warmth of the summer, we made tents with old sheets and Gran's clothes maiden, which collapsed as we settled inside ... We picnicked with our dolls and dozed in the dappled sunlight, soothed by the contented murmur of bees ... In the early autumn we loved the misty harvest mornings when the trees, laden with their luscious, ripe fruit gave up their treasure ... the smoky smell of rich autumn earth and the pungent perfume of the ripe fruit will warm my memory forever.

Picnics and orchards often go hand in hand and a few orchards even doubled up as tea gardens, with restful deck chairs and low tables adding to the relaxed atmosphere. The Orchard Tea Gardens in Grantchester near Cambridge are a particularly charming example. Planted in 1868, the orchard became a tea garden in the spring of 1897 after a group of Cambridge students asked the owner of Orchard House if they could have tea in the blossoming orchard, rather than on the front lawn. The idea was an instant success and since then generations of students have made the pleasant 3-mile journey by foot, bike or punt from Cambridge to Grantchester to enjoy a relaxing, rural tea.

The Orchard Tea Gardens at Grantchester have provided teas to Cambridge University students and other guests for over a hundred years.

Orchards were often the setting or at least the excuse for country celebrations. As far back as the Middle Ages, cherry fairs were an essential part of the yearly calendar of events. These usually took place at harvest time, known as 'Cherrytime', but some celebrations also focused on the blossom season. In the cherry orchards of Kent, a ceremony known as 'Blessing the Orchard' would take place on a Sunday in early May as part of Evensong. The congregation would walk to the orchard in full bloom and watch the vicar bless the trees, in a tradition that has its origins in pagan times.

The most famous orchard tradition was the wassail – a word which comes from the Old English 'waes hael' meaning 'be healthy'. The ceremony, which usually took place on Twelfth Night, aimed at bringing good health to the orchard and the guarantee of an abundant crop the following year. Loud noises – from shot guns, drums, whistles, the clanging of pans and pots, as well as singing – were designed to repel evil spirits and wake up the trees from their winter slumber, while a tree in the orchard (usually the oldest) was showered in cider. Sometimes the trunk of the tree was beaten with

This atmospheric nineteenth-century print shows the wassailing of apple trees with cider in a Devonshire orchard on Twelfth Night.

THE WASSAIL BOWL

During Christmas the wassail bowl, containing a mixture of wine, ale, sugar, spices, eggs and apples, would be taken from house to house. Householders were expected to give money in return for a sip of the drink and the promise of good health the following year.

sticks – a symbolic gesture designed to encourage the sap to flow up the tree. Cider-soaked toast and cakes were hung from its branches, acting as pagan offerings to the tree. As part of the ceremony, villagers would drink mulled cider and serenade the trees with the Wassail song, which went something like this:

Old Apple Tree, we wassail thee
And hoping thou wilt bear
Hatfuls, capfuls, three bushel bagfuls
And a little heap under the stairs
Hip! Hip! Hooray!

Other superstitious rituals were associated with orchards, particularly apple orchards. At harvest time, it was not uncommon for pickers to leave a few fruit on the trees as offerings to the spirits. This, it was hoped, would ensure a good crop the following year, but if the fruits were still on the tree in the spring this spelled bad luck. During the winter months, it was common to give an apple, 'dressed' with cloves, holly, nuts and other natural features, to friends and family members as a symbol of health and good fortune.

Nowadays, pagan superstitions have largely disappeared but some ancient orchard-related traditions, particularly wassailing, are being revived, thanks in no small part to the Save our Orchards Campaign, launched in 1989 by the charity Common Ground. As we shall see in the next and final chapter, a vigorous movement to reclaim old or dying orchards, to establish new ones, and to create communities and events around these precious places has been steadily growing.

BROAD OAK
COMMUNITY ORCHARD

This small nature reserve, nearly half an acre, lies just south of Sturminster Newton on the outskirts of Broad Oak.

One of few traditional orchards remaining in the area.

Dorset Trust ha[s] owned orchard 1979 a[nd] today succes[s] manage[s] the "lo[cal] Commu[nity] with s...

WILLOW WARBLER

LONG EARED BAT

.. AND THE COCKCHAFER FLIES AT NIGHT .

IN THE SUMMER

· ON SUMMER NIGHTS THE ORCHARD IS AN IDEAL HUNTING GROUND FOR THE LITTLE OWL ...

BULLFINCHES

LITTLE OWL

IN THE SPRING

· APPLE BLOSSOM ATTRACTS BIRDS AND INSECTS FOR FOOD AND BEES FOR POLLINATION ·

APPLES ARE ASSOCIATED WITH POMONA, AN AUTUMN DEITY. THIS FESTIVAL IS PROBABLY NOW HALLOWE'EN, INCLUDING THE TRADITION OF APPLE BOBBING

ADAM AND EVE WERE TEMPTED BY AN APPLE "THE FRUIT OF KNOWLEDGE" IN THE GARDEN OF EDEN

'AN APPLE A DAY KEEPS THE DOCTOR AWAY'!

ISAAC NEWTON 'DISCOVERED' GRAVITY AFTER WATCHING AN APPLE FALL

· LEAVES PROVIDE FOOD FOR CATERPILLARS AND LADYBIRDS, WHO FEED ON THE APHIDS ·

· BARK IS IDEAL CAMOUFLAGE MATERIAL FOR THE EYED HAWK MOTH AND A HABITAT FOR FEEDING TREECREEPERS ·

HOLES IN THE TRUNK ATTRACT ROOSTING LONG-EARED BATS AND NESTING BLUE TITS ·

TWO RARE APPLE SPECIES HAVE BEEN IDENTIFIED IN THE ORCHARD: AUTUMN PERMAIN & KING GEORGE V

OLD APPLE VARIETIES FROM DORSET INCLUDE MELCOMBE RUSSET AND TYNEHAM APPLE

IN THE 1980'S NEW TREES WERE PLANTED, INCLUDING:

EYED HAWK MOTH

LONG EARED BAT

· A FLOWER-RICH GRASSLAND IN SPRING AND SUMMER, SUPPORTING MANY OF DORSET'S NOTABLE SPECIES ·

WOOD ANEMONE

SAW-WORT

OX-EYE DAISY

TREECREEPER

ALEXANDER SPEEDWELL

DEVILS BIT SCABIOUS

COMMON KNAPWEED

IN THE AUTUMN

· FALLEN FRUIT PROVIDES A FEAST FOR MANY BIRDS AND INSECTS AS WELL AS BADGERS AND HEDGEHOGS ·

· DEAD WOOD ATTRACTS THE RUBY-TAILED WASP AND MANY SPECIES OF BEETLE ·

FIELDFARE

REDWING

LESSER STAG BEETLE

RED ADMIRALS

WASP

APPLE FRUIT
· is used in cooking for making cakes and jam ... and the juice for cider and vinegar ..

HEDGEHOG

CODLIN MOTH CATERPILLAR

MISTLETOE

APPLE WOOD
· the cogs for the watermill at Sturminster Newton are made of apple wood ... this timber has many uses including mallet-making and is excellent for smoking foods ..

BLACKBIRD

WASSAILING
- a mid winter tradition to protect trees from evil spirits and to ensure a plentiful crop. Evil spirits were driven away by beating or rapping the tree trunks ..

IN THE WINTER

~ **APPLE DAY IS CELEBRATED ON OCTOBER 21st EACH YEAR** ~

[...] OAK [COM]MUNITY ORCHARD [STUR]MINSTER NEWTON [...]ET ·

Supported by the
Heritage Lottery Fund

Dorset Wildlife Trust

A FRUITFUL FUTURE?

ACCORDING to the National Trust, 60 per cent of Britain's orchards have disappeared since the 1950s. In the last twenty years or so, however, initiatives have been launched to stem this downward trend.

A turning point was Apple Day, held on 21 October 1990 in Covent Garden. Organised by the charity Common Ground, this 'pomological celebration' was designed to highlight the variety of apples grown in Britain and revive an interest in growing, eating and cooking Britain's national fruit. From this one event, hundreds of others followed. Apple days and weekends are now held annually across the country, in orchards, historic gardens, villages, museums and cider mills. Activities include orchard walks, apple and juice tastings, apple identification services, pruning workshops, the sale of apple-related produce such as apple cake, chutneys and juices, cider-making demonstrations, exhibitions, games such as apple bobbing and 'apple-and-spoon' races, and the longest apple peel competitions. Pomologists are sometimes on hand to identify apples brought in by visitors, which can lead to the re-appearance of a long-lost variety, as was the case of the apple Red Rollo, re-discovered during a Cornish Apple Day in 1991. Apple Day has almost become a secular harvest festival. Its establishment is certainly helping to revive an interest in local apples and highlight the importance of local, traditionally managed orchards.

Old-fashioned cherry fairs are also experiencing a renaissance, as can be seen at the Museum of East Anglian Life in Stowmarket, where the Suffolk Cherry Fair – an annual celebration during the eighteenth and nineteenth centuries – was revived in 2003. Similarly, Pershore's traditional 'Plum Fayre', which in the 1920s advertised itself as 'The Largest Plum Show on Earth', was resurrected in 1996. It is now known as the Pershore Plum Festival and takes place in August. In Cumbria, the Westmorland Damson Association was formed in 1996 to preserve the damson orchards of the old county of Westmorland; it holds a Damson Day every April. Many more such events are held throughout the country to celebrate local orchard fruits.

Opposite:
Broad Oak
Community
Orchard is run by
the Dorset
Wildlife Trust, who
commissioned this
poster from local
artist Antonia
Phillips.

Local apples being displayed at the Apple and Cider Fair at Eggersford Garden and Country Centre in Devon. The apples were exhibited by Orchards Live, a charity that helps to save orchards in North Devon.

Far right:
A 'longest apple peel' competition is held annually at Ely Apple Festival, East Anglia's biggest apple celebration.

The desire to stop the decline of traditional orchards has also led, on a county level, to the creation of orchard groups keen to revive local fruit varieties. The Gloucestershire Orchards Group, for instance, was founded in 2001 with the aim of conserving, promoting and celebrating traditional orchards in the county. Its establishment was the culmination of research by experts who in 1991 undertook the first ever survey of the county's orchards and demonstrated just how bad the situation really was (over 75 per cent of Gloucestershire's orchards have been lost in the last fifty years). Thanks to this research, in 1992 a 'Restoring our Landscape' grant was made available which has financed the planting of over three thousand orchard trees. Local varieties have been identified and grafted and a Museum Apple Orchard was planted at Brookthorpe, near Gloucester, now home to the Gloucestershire Orchards Group, and a centre for orchard training and rural skills.

In 2010, over 17,000 people attended Pershore's Plum Festival – an annual celebration during which visitors can, amongst other things, sample plum sausages, sweets, jams and other related produce.

Significantly, in 2007, traditional orchards were designated as a 'Priority Habitat' under the UK Government's Biodiversity Action Plan. In 2009, the National Trust, together with other organisations including Natural England and the Wildlife Trusts, launched a project to 'improve the condition and increase the extent of traditional orchards throughout England'. Staff at a number of National Trust sites, including Beningbrough Hall in North Yorkshire, Smallhythe Place in Kent, Brockhampton Estate in Herefordshire, and Cotehele in Cornwall, have overseen the restoration of old orchards and the establishment of new ones, undertaken orchard surveys, and organised awareness-raising events as well as training and workshops.

One of the biggest of these projects involved the planting of a new Mother Orchard at Cotehele in the Tamar Valley, an area known for its apple and cherry orchards and its long tradition of market gardening. The 13-acre orchard was planted in 2007/2008. Featuring over 120 different varieties of Cornish and Devonshire apples, it will act, according to the Trust, as a 'gene bank of local varieties'.

Other organisations have been taking similar steps to safeguard local fruit varieties. In 2010 an orchard was planted in the grounds of Fife Agricultural College to save Scotland's ancient fruit varieties, which include the 400-year-old 'Arbroath Pippin' and the Victorian cooker 'Stirling Castle'. In Knucklas on the Welsh border, an orchard featuring eighty-six Welsh heirloom cultivars was planted. It includes the elusive 'Bardsey Apple', which according to apple expert Joan Morgan is the rarest apple in the world.

Perhaps the most encouraging aspect of the recent 'orchard revival' is the rise in the number of community orchards. Whether located in a city, town or village, community orchards are increasingly acting as outdoor hubs for local communities: here people can meet; enjoy picnics, open-air plays, talks and poetry readings; attend picking and grafting days and special fruit-related events; and survey or simply delight in the flora and fauna. At the heart of every community orchard is a group of enthusiastic and committed people who want to make a difference in their local area. Community orchards are not strictly about the production of fruit, although this is of course a wonderful by-product. It is about enriching communities and introducing biodiversity into local areas. Journalist, chef and 'real food' campaigner Hugh Fearnley-Whittingstall recently wrote: 'The idea of community orchards is so good, so obviously right, that I think it's fair to describe it as vital.' The interest in community orchards has increased to such an extent in recent years that a special *Community Orchards Handbook* is now available, which explains exactly how to go about setting up your own.

Even in the heart of London, steps are being taken to map surviving fruit trees, rejuvenate old orchard sites and create new ones. Since its foundation in 2009, the London Orchard Project has identified 45 acres of land in

Salthaven
Community
Orchard in Essex
has a range of
apple and pear
trees dating back
to the 1960s and
the 1990s. Areas of
long grass are kept
un-mown to
encourage insects
such as crickets
and grasshoppers.

London where former orchards were located. The organisation helps restore old orchards and plant new ones. It also trains volunteer 'orchard leaders' to manage the plots and organises special events such as juicing and cider-making workshops.

Knowing where traditional orchards are located, as well as their age and condition, is of course vital for their conservation. An initiative by the People's Trust for Endangered Species (PTES) has recently produced an inventory of England's traditional orchards using aerial photography. The inventory combined already existing survey data with these new aerial photographs to form a resource upon which all future conservation can be based. Researchers have located 35,378 traditional orchards across fifty-one

Apples are piled
and ready to be
pressed at the
award-winning
Somerset Cider
Brandy Company.

counties, or the equivalent of 42,000 acres. The analysis revealed that just 9 per cent of England's traditional orchards are in excellent condition, while 46 per cent are in good condition and 45 per cent in bad condition.

In order to survive and thrive, orchards need to serve a purpose and be looked after. Whether as a community orchard or as productive plots, they need to be managed in new and imaginative ways that suit the requirements of today's society and, as much as possible, involve local people. At the National Trust's Brockhampton Estate in Herefordshire, for instance, visitors are invited to participate in the picking of the damsons, which are then made into special 'Brockhampton Brand' damson preserves. In Devon, Orchard Link was established in 1998 to support, advise and train small orchard owners and also, importantly, to help them find outlets for their produce. There are other similar local and regional initiatives designed to help smaller orchardists. One example is the Big Apple Association, which brings together the seven parishes of the Marcle Ridge in Herefordshire: Aylton, Little Marcle, Much Marcle, Munsley, Pixley, Putley and Woolhope. Twice a year – at blossom time and harvest time – the association holds a celebration of local apple and pear orchards, during which local growers can sell and promote their produce.

Locally made, heritage cider and perry are enjoying a revival, not just in the West Country, but in other parts of England as well as Wales and Scotland. Waulkmill Cider, for instance, uses only apples grown in Dumfries and Galloway and the company is planning to plant more orchards of traditional Scottish varieties in the region.

Other producers are reaping the rewards of specialising in high-end products, such as the Somerset Cider Brandy Company, creator of Alchemy, a fifteen-year-old brandy that currently sells for £30 a bottle. In 2011 the company was granted European Union Protected Geographical Indication status, which means that its brandy has the same protection as champagne.

Such companies, projects and events offer hope for the future of Britain's orchards, so that we, like William Lawson almost four hundred years ago, can still enjoy all that is to be gained from them. As he so beautifully wrote in *A New Orchard and Garden*: 'What can your eye desire to see, your eares to hear, your mouth to taste, or your nose to smell, that is not to be had in an orchard?'

This 1880s painting, *Girls Collecting Apples*, by Jane Mary Dealy, captures the romance, beauty and fruitful harvest that can be enjoyed in an old orchard.

FURTHER READING

Bracey, G. *Apple Games and Customs*. Common Ground, 1994.

Copas, L. *A Somerset Pomona: The Cider Apples of Somerset*. Dovecote Press, 2001.

Gee, M. *Mazzards: The Revival of the Curious North Devon Cherry*. The Mint Press, 2004.

Greenoak, F. *Forgotten Fruit: The English Orchard and Fruit Garden*. Andre Deutsch, 1983.

Greenoak, F. *Fruit and Vegetable Gardens*. The National Trust, 1990.

Keech, D. *The Common Ground Book of Orchards*. Common Ground, 2000.

King, A. and Clifford, S. *The Apple Source Book*. Hodder & Stoughton, 2007.

King, A. and Clifford, S. *The Community Orchards Handbook*. Green Books, 2011.

Major, A. *Cherries in the Rise: Cherry Cultivation in Kent*. S.B. Publications, 1997.

Morgan, J. *The New Book of Apples: The Definitive Guide to over 2000 Varieties*. Ebury Press, 2002.

Quinion, M. B. *Cidermaking*. Shire, 2008.

Roach, F. A. *Cultivated Fruits of Britain: Their Origin and History*. Wiley-Blackwell, 1985.

Russell, J. *Man-made Eden: Historic Orchards in Somerset and Gloucestershire*. Redcliffe Press, 2007.

Sanders, Rosie. *The Apple Book*. Frances Lincoln, 2007.

Spiers, V. *Burcombes, Queenies and Colloggetts*. West Brendon, 1996.

Twiss, S. *Apples: A Social History*. National Trust, 1999.

PLACES TO VISIT

Acorn Bank, Temple Sowerby, near Penrith, Cumbria CA10 1SP.
   Telephone: 01768 361893. Website: www.nationaltrust.org.uk
Barrington Court, Barrington, near Ilminster, Somerset TA19 0NQ
   Telephone: 01460 242614. Website: www.nationaltrust.org.uk
Beningbrough Hall & Gardens, Beningbrough, York, North Yorkshire
   YO30 1DD.
   Telephone: 01904 472027. Website: www.nationaltrust.org.uk
Berrington Hall, near Leominster, Herefordshire HR6 0DW.
   Telephone: 01568 615721. Website: www.nationaltrust.org.uk
Brogdale Horticultural Trust, Brogdale Road, Faversham, Kent ME13
   8XZ. Telephone: 01795 536250. Website: www.brogdale.org
Cornish Cyder Farm, Penhallow, Truro, Cornwall TR4 9LW.
   Telephone: 01872 573356. Website: www.thecornishcyderfarm.co.uk
Cotehele, St Dominick, near Saltash, Cornwall PL12 6TA.
   Telephone: 01579 351346. Website: www.nationaltrust.org.uk
Felbrigg Hall, Norwich, Norfolk NR11 8PR.
   Telephone: 01263 837444. Website: www.nationaltrust.org.uk
Fenton House, Hampstead Grove, Hampstead NW3 6SP.
   Telephone: 020 7435 3471. Website: www.nationaltrust.org.uk
Hughenden Manor, High Wycombe, HP14 4LA.
   Telephone: 01494 755573. Website: www.nationaltrust.org.uk
Perry's Cider Mills, Dowlish Wake, Ilminster, Somerset TA19 0NY.
   Telephone: 01460 55195. Website: www.perryscider.co.uk
Snowshill Manor, Snowshill, near Broadway, Gloucestershire WR12 7JU
   Telephone: 01386 852410. Website: www.nationaltrust.org.uk
Stanley Lord Orchard, Shenley Park, Radlett Lane, Shenley, Hertfordshire,
   WD7 9DW.
   Telephone: 01923 852629. Website: www.shenleypark.co.uk
Tatton Park, Knutsford, Cheshire, WA16 6QN.
   Telephone: 01625 374400. Website: www.tattonpark.org.uk
Tewin Orchard, 1 Upper Green, Tewin, Welwyn AL6 0LX. Email:
   mike@tewinorchard.co.uk. Website: www.tewinorchard.co.uk
Tidnor Wood Orchard Trust.
   Telephone: 01369 840360. Website: www.tidnorwood.org.uk
Tresillian House, Tresillian, Newquay, Cornwall TR8 4PS.
   Telephone: 01637 877447. Website: www.tresillian-house.co.uk
West Dean Gardens, West Dean, Chichester PO18 0QZ.
   Telephone: 01243 811301. Website: www.westdean.org.uk
RHS Garden Wisley, Woking, Surrey GU23 6QB.
   Telephone: 01483 224234. Website: www.rhs.org.uk

INDEX